ONE DAY AT SHIRLEY'S . . .

Poems by Seven Writers:

Ruth Linsley Forman
Marian Goldner
E. Jane Johanson
Shirley Kirshner
Florence Lever
Joanne Niswander
Winston Smith

HEATHERDOWN PRESS

© Copyright **HEATHERDOWN PRESS** 1986

ISBN 0-9610038-1-2

Manufactured in the United States of America

Published by HEATHERDOWN PRESS
3450 BRANTFORD ROAD
TOLEDO, OHIO

All Rights Reserved

FORE WORD

One day at Shirley's, six lovers of words sat around the table, doing what wordsmiths love most--sharing their work. Encouraged by a growing list of publications and prizes, they decided to band together for a joint publication of their poetry. A seventh poet-friend, 103 years old and still writing, was invited to join the group. That was the beginning.

Now, some months and many meetings later, you hold the result. May our collection of words and works bring as much joy to you, our readers, as they have to us, their creators.

Ruth Linsley Forman Shirley Kirshner
Marian Goldner   Florence Lever
E. Jane Johanson   Joanne Niswander
Winston Smith

30 Rockefeller Plaza
New York, NY 10112
212 664-5488

A Division of
National Broadcasting
Company, Inc.

Willard Scott
TODAY

NBC NEWS

December 1, 1986

E. Jane Johanson
2513 Ashborne Place
Toledo, Ohio 43606

Dear Ms. Johanson:

Florence Lever may be 103 years old, but her poetry is as fresh as tomorrow.

I enjoyed all your writings and hope you continue your inspirational work.

Love, and all best wishes.

Willard Scott

CONTENTS

Ruth Linsley Forman

Day Lilies - 1
A Different Dragon - 2
Giraffes - 3
A Snake - 4
Deermouse - 4
The Owl - 5
Water Lily - 5
Fire Truck - 6
March - 6
October - 7
On Halloween Night - 7
Halloween - 8
Snowman - 8

Marian Goldner

Eden Lost - 9
Camryn - 10
Haiku - 11, 12
Bred To Serve - 13
Ruins - 14
The Speaker - 15
After Class - 16
Observations - 17
Freida - 18
My Choice - 19
Limericks - 20

E. Jane Johanson

    Lincoln's Monument At Midnight - 21
    84 Charing Cross Road - 22, 23
    Ben Jonson, Westminster Abbey - 24, 25
    The Flock - 26
    The Chrysalis - 27
    Night Comes On - 28
    Kurt Vonnegut Tells It All To You - 29
    The Poets' Fellowship - 30
    The Apology - 31
    The Raspberry Patch - 32
    Someone You Should Know - 33
    Bad Language - 34, 35

Shirley Kirshner

    Dissidents - 36
    Kinship Of The Successful - 37
    Like A Pekinese - 38
    Artichokes And Rutabagas - 39
    Pythia - 40
    A Bug - 41
    Relative Age - 42
    It Is Not True - 43
    A New Year - 44
    Chronology - 44
    Chapel Royal - 45, 46
    Walk The Jewish Quarter - 47
    Dimensions - 48

Florence Lever

    Our 50th State - 49
    Haiku - 50, 51, 52
    Southport - 53

Joanne Niswander

    Monument To Madison Avenue - 54
    Moving Sale - 55
    Gillies Hill, Vermont - 56
    The Inn At Yesterday Corner - 57
    Nursing Home: Ma Mère - 58
    Nursing Home: Through A Glass, Darkly - 59
    The Greening - 60
    Winter Woods - 61
    A Child's Garden of Vegetables - 62, 63
    Make Mine Tutti Fruitti - 64, 65
    Case 13 (Brown vs. Green) - 66
    If Noses Could Hear - 67

Winston Smith

    Old Man And The Ants - 68
    The Wind - 69
    Fly In Amber - 70, 71
    Two Juncoes Flew - 72
    True Poet - 73
    Flashback - 74
    Old Canal Houses - 75, 76
    Dusty Answer - 77
    Sing Johnny One Note - 78
    Damsel Flies Are Found - 79
    Element Of Purple - 80
    Day With Apples - 81

RUTH LINSLEY FORMAN

Ruth Linsley Forman taught kindergarten and first grade for many years, so it is not surprising her poems appeal to the imaginations of young children. Her Halloween poems appeared in INSTRUCTOR magazine. Now that she is retired she expects future writing to express a broadening range of interests and experience.

DAY LILIES*

Frail figure bent
in summer's cotton dress,
her fingers cup each golden throated flower
whose fragrance trumpets
to the waiting bees.

Mindful of their single day of grace,
she plucks spent blooms of yesterday,
puts them aside just as each day
she sheds the worries of the past,
seeing beauty all around
this perfect time that comes before the last.

*The lilies are Martha's - age 92

A DIFFERENT DRAGON

There was once a dragon who, indeed, was very strange.
He did not roar at people if they strayed upon his range,
Nor open up his dragon mouth to shoot out smoke or flame,
Or lash his tail, or flash his eyes, or seem at all untame.
Instead he put his claws up to his lips and uttered, "Sh-h-h!"
Then tiptoed down his dragon path, disturbing not a bush.

He said, "Sh-h-h!"
He said, "Sh-h-h!
Don't make a single sound!"
He said, "Sh-h-h!"
He said, "Sh-h-h!"
As he crept along the ground.

Then all who saw him on his way began to follow, too,
So curious were all of them to see what he might do.
He reached his lair then turned around
   and searched within his vest.
He pulled out gum and candy hearts
   to give to every guest.
Then everyone said "Thank you, Sir," in whispers soft and low,
They backed away politely when it seemed the time to go.
The dragon took his kerchief out. He waved to one and all,
But put his claws back to his lips when they began to call.

He said, "Sh-h-h!"
He said, "Sh-h-h
Don't make a single sound!"
He said, "Sh-h-h!
He said "Sh-h-h!"
As with a single bound

He went into his dragon house, then bolted fast the door,
And all the folk who stood there saw the dragon never more.

GIRAFFES

Giraffes have necks
That reach so high,
They bump their heads
Against the sky.

What is slim
    And has no feet?
What cannot sit
    Upon a seat?

What has no legs
    To run away,
But when you come
    It will not stay?

What goes so fast
    Across the grass,
Not you nor I
    Can see him pass?

    A SNAKE!

DEERMOUSE

I can't think why they call this mouse a deer.
He has no antlers, and his tail is long.
His legs conclude in paws and not in hooves,
And therefore, I believe they named him wrong.

THE OWL

No rear view mirror
Has the owl
Who sits up in his tree.
But then, he has
No need of one,
For when he wants to see
What goes behind him
Out of sight,
He turns his neck and head
So when you see
The front of him,
You see the back, instead.

WATER LILY

A water lily's feet are wet,
Its collar green and dry.
Its face, all pink and petaled,
Can only see the sky.

FIRE TRUCK

F is the fighting fire truck
Painted in flaming red.
    When signals blast
    It follows fast
While the chief flies on ahead.

Buses pull to the curbing
At the siren's furious cry,
    For early or late
    They have to wait,
While the fire truck flashes by.

MARCH

Will march come in like a lamb,
Or come like a lion, roaring?
Will it bring sun and daisy wheels,
Or send our kites up soaring?

OCTOBER

I know you well, October.
Your nights are black as death.
And though your days are amber,
You breathe a hoary breath.

ON HALLOWEEN NIGHT

Let's fly like a bat on Halloween night,
And give the people a terrible fright!

    Or creep through the dark like a big black cat,
    And make the people cry, "What's that?"

Or float like a ghost on the midnight air
To make the people all beware!

    Or zoom on a broom like the witches ride,
    And make the people run and hide!

But when the witching hour is done,
We'll tell them all it was Halloween fun!

HALLOWEEN

Witches, ghosts and bats are seen
Out at night on Halloween.

Boys and girls with scary faces
Peer at me from spooky places.

Everything looks very queer
This jack-o-lantern time of year!

SNOWMAN

I made a snowman
On the lawn.
By afternoon
He was nearly gone.

At first he stood
Quite tall and fat.
The sun came out
And that was that!

Now all that's left
Is in a pile,
His hat and broom,
His eyes and smile.

MARIAN GOLDNER

Marian Goldner, who signs her children's books "Grandma Marian", has been writing creatively since she was in fourth grade. She has had published everything from magazine articles, poetry, stories, and books to plays, and has won prizes in almost every field. Her latest book, GEORGIE THE JOVIAL GIRAFFE, written in lyrical rhyme for children, won International First Prize at a competition in Budapest, Hungary. Though she loves all kinds of literature, Grandma Marian has become "curiouser and curiouser" about poetry and its evolution in her lifetime.

EDEN LOST

He slithered through the summer night
Up the tree to its highest height.
In the morn, when Eve came into sight
Said he to her, "Just take one bite."

When Eve observed, with great delight,
This big red apple, shining bright
There was in her no thought of fright,
So quickly, she took one great big bite.

Then Adam, who was erudite
Observed his wife in dread and fright.
He knew full well the wrong from right
And yet, he too took one big bite.

The skies grew dark and lightning white
Flashed 'cross the skies; 'twas dark as night,
And thus began the human plight
When the snake lured Eve to take one big bite.

CAMRYN

Wide brown eyes
Sending messages of fear,
She steps lightly in my presence
As though danger were near

Keeping my distance
I speak carefully
My tone light
Lest she suddenly
Dart into the night

Her home is all nature
She longs to live free
Smell the wild flowers
Sleep under trees

White water rivers
Rocky terrain
She dances with joy
To nature's refrain

When man encroaches
Her idyllic home
She seeks deeper forests
In which to roam

Flesh of my flesh
Core of my core
Some capricious muse
Placed the heart of a doe
In this child I bore.

HAIKU

The sun slips away
We bathe in its afterglow
A luminous blush

Lazily swimming
Goldfish glide through clear waters
Dazzling sea jewels

A field of daisies
Colorful cushion to lure
The searching honeybee

Peeking through soft snow
A crocus warms our hearts
With April springshine

Is it an ogre,
A fierce and fiery dragon?
No, only driftwood

Caterpillar crawls
With many feet; yet so slow
Fuzzy hair bristling

HAIKU

Along the seashore
Wavelets splash across my feet
Wash away the undersand

A hot summer day
Horse flies buzzing noisily
Over a candy kiss

Sharp icicles point
Silver lances, threatening
The innocent snow

The roaring lion
Mighty king of the jungle
Hides from the lightning

BRED TO SERVE

What's inside?
That head held high,
Nodding, smiling, controlled
White-gloved hand waving

Eyes must not meet

Steps down gracefully from ornate carriage
Solemn, serene in great church
Clear-voiced
Regally humble

Commands performances
Greets dignitaries
Christens ships
Rides fine horses with elegant skill

Queen of all the British Empire
Waves from the balcony

But what's inside?

RUINS

Facing each other
across a space of a hundred feet or so,
two stone lions,
chipped, eroded
by centuries of sandstorms
serenely guard what is no more.

Can you hear?
trumpets blaring,
armor-clad soldiers marching,
little men, from another age.

The monarch
perched on his gilded throne
archly surveys his troops as they pass.
His pampered wife
is pleased to be observed, envied, admired.

Timeless desert winds
sweep back and forth,
whip the guardian lions,
carry echoes
of ever-present war games.

THE SPEAKER

Eagerly
    we simple folk gather
    to listen to the golden
    words of the famous author

Pedantically
    he approaches the podium

Raptly
    we listen
    as he dangles phrases so wise
    so scholarly that I cannot
    grasp their meanings

```
                    apple
              juicy
       a red,                    reach
Like                     quite
                 I can't
              high
          so
    a   branch
On
```

AFTER CLASS

Poets
Artists
Class is over.
Over there's a field of clover
Wild flowers spilt upon the leas
Lit by sunlight through the trees

Daisies, lilies, goldenrod,
Nature's canvas
Signed by God

OBSERVATIONS

What's ambition to one
Is sloth to another
He's a bum to his boss
And a king to his mother!

Men unload their building tools,
Handle them like precious jewels.
Cannot hammer, saw or wire
'Less the radio's turned up higher.

Wiggly minnows, hundreds strong
Bigger fishy comes along,
Gobbles many down complete--
He's the snapper that WE eat!

FREIDA

I am cut
she bleeds,
Delights in my good fortune,
knows not ego

What she knows
is to give and to care

She is hurt
I weep
She is happy
I rejoice
Dear to me as life

My sistermother

MY CHOICE

To dig in rubble
of another man's dream
from an age I never knew,
intrude upon
his long-buried life
is something I'd love to do

Learn how he cooked and clothed himself,
Did he sing to his love, bring her gifts?
Did he trade? Was he skilled?
Was he fat? Was he thin?
The tale's under sand where it drifts.

Oh, a pick, a spade, a shovel, a broom
On a far off ancient shore
That's what I'd choose
just turn me loose
I'd stay there forever more!

LIMERICKS

A baldheaded man from Rangoon
Said "Fortune will smile on me soon!"
So he sat by the sea
Like a wealthy grandee
And was lost in a tropic typhoon

A Quaker exceedingly chaste
Viewed all sorts of dance with distaste
But when Nuryev came through
She put on a tutu
And danced off with his arm 'round her waist

A maid of the streets known as Gwen
Became deathly allergic to men
So she ceased fornication
Took a Danish vacation
Now everyone's calling her Ben

E. JANE JOHANSON

E. Jane Johanson is a native of Scotland, graduate of Edinburgh University, author of LOVING, LEAVING AND LIVING AGAIN (1980), co-author of SPIRITS AND SEASONS (1982), recipient of awards in national and international competitions. Her poems have been published in various magazines and in the Ohio Poetry Day Annuals, THE BEST OF 1983, 1984, 1985, and 1986.

LINCOLN'S MONUMENT AT MIDNIGHT

Tonight it's quiet,
as Abraham was,
only one shadow
moves on the marble coat.

A woman comes
out of the cold-slow-moving dark,
into the light
to hear him say again,
"One nation indivisible."

Listen,
a woman's voice is singing, "America."
This showcase was her choice.
She would stand beside him,
confident that he would understand.

A prophet-voice is telling of a dream
that rose above the pool,
the obelisk, circled the world,
a dream that Lincoln shared.

Other ghosts crowd in,
watching the light on the marble coat
and the shadow,
a picture in black and white.

THE BOOKSHOP AT 84 CHARING CROSS ROAD

It's dim inside, yet intimate.
I cannot yet articulate the smell.
It blends the must and dust
of aged books with oak of walls and floor.

A stand-up desk, a work-lamp on it.
A clerk with Hogarth nose
looks up and says, "Good afternoon.
You've come to browse. Please do."

The shelves go up and up,
up to the ceiling,
old and kind and grey,
as if the oak had breathed on it
a hundred years
to make perpetual dusk.

First-prints are under glass,
Cruikshank, Rackham, Spy,
illustrators too
illustrious I'm sure.

If I should choose a book
by Charles Lamb, Isaak Walton say
or Quiller-Couch, I'd cease to browse.

I'd walk with Elizabethans
where they walked,
explore the Hellespont,
learn more of Hector and the Trojan War.

The kindly clerk
would have to move my way
to say, "Madam, it's nearly six."

BEN JONSON, WESTMINSTER

In days of yore
the men who would be great
must claim entitlement and pay for space
among the men who lie in crypts
beneath the Abbey floor.

The great and nearly-great
are buried here,
their names and dates and eulogies
are written clear.
They lie in marble crypts beneath the floor.

Ben knew all this
and went to claim his space
and pay the fee,
to be forever with the blest
who lie in crypts, no less, beneath the floor.

His purse was slim that day,
he could not pay the treasurer.
Did Ben evade,
or did he think he'd paid to rest
in treasured crypt beneath the Abbey floor?

With pomp and panoply and tears
they gave poor Ben, now well-advanced in years,
his last entitlement,
rest among the best
who lie in crypts beneath the Abbey floor.

Poor Ben was left in trusted hands
the sexton and the sexton's man.
The treasurer was there to see
that only those who paid the fee
would lie in crypts beneath the Abbey floor.

The precious space would be reserved
for great men who deserved the best.
He would not let
a dead-beat in to rest
in marble crypt beneath the Abbey floor.

He'd stand him up against the wall,
though Ben was just a little tall,
reserve the horizontal space,
the precious and eternal place,
a marble crypt beneath the Abbey floor.

And if the story sounds untrue
and just a little tall to you,
let history give the actual date
when workmen came to where Ben stood
against the wall, beneath the Abbey floor.

They saw the horizontal place
and slid John Hunter in the space.
Poor Ben stood by without a word
for eloquence might sound absurd,
among the best, beneath the Abbey floor .

In fact, he seemed a bit aloof,
his red hair pressed against the roof,
while all the rest
were laid to rest among the best
in marble crypts beneath the Abbey floor.

THE FLOCK
(IN THE SCOTTISH HIGHLANDS)

Slowly they pass
onto the grass made grey with dew,
leave the road
that I must take alone.

They have no musts,
are free to go and come
on sheep-worn paths.

They have no loneliness
following sheep that go before
through heather, in and out,
stopping to crop or bite a bit of gorse.

They are the hundredth flock,
of flocks that stay the same.
The solitary one that lies
close to the dry stone wall,

must be the self-same ewe,
the iris-eyed,
I saw against that dyke
when I was young.

Does she dream droves of sheep
that feed on air,
watching clouds
that scud away from her?

THE CHRYSALIS

Hilda is free.
She has crawled from her narrow space
into the light.

She has stopped
moving like a man-out-of-work
guilty, humbled, hopeless,
life hanging like a frayed cloth.

Someone has told her
her breasts are delectable.
She has bought a sheer blouse
to show her possessions.

Her voice is stronger,
her ideas are held with conviction.
Loved for herself, she is bursting out
leaving the wrappings behind.

NIGHT COMES ON

He taught her touch and sense
and nakedness of heart and mind,
her true contemporary.
She let him bend her will
incline her ways.

He was her God,
conscience, absolver, priest,
and when he left she waited,
waited and cried,

cried out
for some absurd forgiveness,
not knowing how to bear the pain
or who would hear.

She drifts
a powerless skiff
without the secrets-of-the-sea.

KURT VONNEGUT TELLS IT ALL TO YOU

Not needed as husband
or father or friend
not able to write as he used to do,
nothing incisively clever for years,
or so it appears.

He wanted an angel
to knock on his door
to spend the days in forgetfulness
in a little nest and explore
the "little death" a little more.

He did not seek honor
for what he had done
but wanted new honor
for just having fun
wrapped in the "little death"

holding a rose to give to his angel,
sans ego, sans clothes.

Glossary: Little death - fleshly delights

THE POETS' FELLOWSHIP

Only lamps are watching
as he walks the long corridors alone,
past mute doors, endlessly seeking
until one opens
and Inspiration walks with him.

He writes what she dictates
on untouched paper,
with a new pen,
before oblivion sets in,

then rests with us,
who listen to the just-discovered words
dictated by Her voice.

THE APOLOGY

There are no roses here today
to welcome you,
to simulate the fragrance
that clings about you, as you move.

Fate guided every thread
laid them down with tender hands,
held and supported them with 100's more,
to make the fabric that is you.

Fear and desire, mastery of self,
the melancholy of experience,
the pain of love
blend in your eyes.

You are in control
of all the intricacy,
warmly human
divinely animal.

No flowers could enhance
the texture of your life,
but roses should have been here
to welcome you.

THE RASPBERRY PATCH

I lean on the morning fence,
see you fuss
over the inventory of growing things.
Your thoughts bridge space
and reach me where I stand

and in the evening
you bring berries,
cradled in your hand.

At your touch
the air is full of unsaid things
that spread like pollen
on the wind.

SOMEONE YOU SHOULD KNOW

Josh is rich,
fabulous looking
with a sense of self,
warm, wry, strong,
adventuresome,
an unclaimed package
of suntan, straight teeth
and charm.

Is he eligible!

BAD LANGUAGE

My mother was gentle, my mother was fair,
but one thing she told me, I must not swear.

I said I'd never do such a thing
but my voice, I am sure, had a curious ring.

And if you wonder what was the cause,
she had not told me what swearing was.

I could not find out, but soon I knew,
that all of my friends had the same rule too.

I lived in a house where they kept that rule,
so I did not learn 'til I went to school.

Then one day a friend with gentle intent
told me exactly what swearing meant.

If you say "Hell-fire," that's bad enough,
but if you leave off the fire, it's even worse.

He was so careful not to be heard,
I wondered what happened if you said that word.

A curious thing then happened to me,
I wanted to try it instantly.

But where could I go, I scratched my head,
and I suddenly thought of the garden shed.

I shut the door, bolted it tight,
looked at the roof, and the little skylight.

I prayed to Jesus, who knew me well,
and asked if he minded if I said, "Hell."

The roof stayed there, the same as before,
so did the window, so did the door.

But my heart was pounding, I didn't feel right,
and I went off to bed real early that night.

But I couldn't sleep, I tossed in bed,
all sorts of troubles passed through my head.

I got up at last, went through to mother,
who happened to be up with my little brother.

What is the trouble, lass, did you have a bad dream?
You're the best little sleeper I've ever seen.

When she said that, I sobbed it all out,
"I swore in the garden shed," at last it was out.

"At whom were you swearing?" my mother said.
Now was a new thought to enter my head.

"Swearing at nobody, nobody heard.
I was locked in the shed when I said that word."

My mother smiled, "This may seem absurd,
but you were not swearing, just saying the word."

She laid her hand on top of my head,
seemed to love me all over, and tucked me in bed.

Down inside, I knew that the Lord
had not minded when I said that word.

SHIRLEY KIRSHNER

The critics all line up to meet her
The Academy surely will seat her
For lines, apt and pleasing
From propitious squeezing
Eleven in pen tan a meter

The above is Shirley's fantasy. She has been published in JEWISH SPECTATOR, GOLDEN GATE REVIEW, ADVENTURES IN POETRY, and OHIO POETRY DAY.

DISSIDENTS

"Yet it does move"
Rebellious words
Galileo
Forfeited Heaven

Psychotic flowers
In nervous fields
Vincent Van Gogh
Distilled madness

In the Gulag
Solzhenitsyn
Caught one snowflake
On his turned up thumb

KINSHIP OF THE SUCCESSFUL

A narrow weak-blue envelope enclosed
Sure proof that she rose high, cream over milk,
And ether over air. Her scattered doubts
Now changed to form one solid weight of pride.
Another mass of ether, glob of cream
Approached, extending liquid hands in brotherhood,
Equality and joy of winning proof
That each existed parallel in life,
And neither stooped to touch each other's spheres.

LIKE A PEKINESE

Like a Pekinese meticulously
Washed and brushed and sprayed
With French perfume, she minces down the street,
Shunning puddles filled with germs and nasty things.
Like a Pekinese contemptuously
Curling up its lip at curs that smell like curs,
She scorns her kind and fixes bulging eyes
Upon a group of godlings claiming
Better blood than homo sapiens can claim.
Like a weary Pekinese, a little breathlessly,
She trips through doors held open by serving hands.
Then, tying satin ribbons round her head,
She sinks into the softly yielding,
Dusty pillow of her mind.

ARTICHOKES AND RUTABAGAS

Bands of ebon tulips, thickly painted,
Covered Minton china underneath.
My table-drumming fingers ached
To scratch the paint and see the plate exposed.
Artichokes are food for patient men,
Satisfied to peel off leaves for nibbles,
Satisfied to seek out subtle tastes.
I ate the artichokes and tasted you,
You, on Minton china spoiled with paint,
You, a food which leaves a man still hungry.
I wanted rutabagas, unadorned, and
Served in bowls of old unpolished pewter.

PYTHIA

I am priestess Pythia at Delphi
Deemed center of the earth by every Greek.
Inside Apollo's sacred temple I
Am the instrument. Through me the gods speak.
For answers to your interrogation
You must feed the sacrificial altars.
Goats' and lambs' blood hones my revelation.
In divine affairs I must not falter.
After I bathe, I chew on laurel leaves,
Drink flagons of wine, breathe volcanic fumes.
I effect my own trance. Still reason cleaves.
Regressed to blackness of an unused womb
I filter wisdom through my mental screen.
Male priests interpret what my ravings mean.

A BUG

One liver-colored juicy-bodied bug,
Wasting power climbing shells and stones and twigs,
Inched its accidental way along the sand
To come beneath my quiet, waiting hand.

I flipped its body over with my thumb
To watch its grasping legs encircle air,
To see its frenzied, undiluted fear,
To know one bug survived because I chose.

RELATIVE AGE

Comfortable,
established,
pyramidal.
On other days he wears
these adjectives easily
as successful men
are wont to do.
Today his mother aged as
Sarah, alone as Hagar
in the desert, waits
for her appointment
with the laser.
Feeling marbles slide
down his trouser pocket,
frog bulging underneath
his shirt, he releases the brake
on her wheelchair,
        begins to
        push
        her
        down
        the
        endless
        corridor.

IT IS NOT TRUE

Children grown,
Husband dead,
It is not true
What's always said.
You can squeeze blood from a turnip,
Soup from a stone.
You can live by bread alone.
Yet if you choose to live apart,
Prepare to starve a hungry heart.

A NEW YEAR

A new year arrives
In an old life
Not with bells
Just a quiet shhh.

CHRONOLOGY

Asses to asses
Lust to lust
Ashes to ashes
Dust to dust
Wife to widow
Widow to crone
Coffin to coffin
Bone to bone.

CHAPEL ROYAL
GRANADA 1978

The same silver crown
We saw in textbooks
When we studied about
Columbus and how
He pleaded with Isabel
To finance his voyages

The same golden coffer
Overflowing with jewels
Legend has it
She scraped to the bottom
To buy three ships
For Christobal Colon

The same silver crown
She wore on her head
That fateful day
When she heeded the advice
Of Torquemada
To expel the Jews

The same golden coffer
Which never knew
The thirty thousand ducats
Fernando was willing to take
To allow the Jews to stay
How Torquemada did scream "Judas"

The same silver crown
She wore on her head
In the Alhambra
While Boabdil lingered
For one last look at his red castle
While his mother chided
"You do well my son
To weep as a women
For the loss of what
You could not defend as a man."

In the Chapel Royal
On a white velvet pillow
Trimmed with gold tassels
The same silver crown
The same golden coffer

WALK THE JEWISH QUARTER
CORDOBA 1978

Walk the Jewish quarter
In the Old City.
Squeeze against the walls,
Salt-white in the sun.
Let the Fathers pass.

Look through the doorways
Into the patios
In the Old City.
Beyond the wrought iron gates,
Lemons hang from branches
Like mobiles stirring on their strings.
Cascading down the balconies,
Carnations spill their red.
Plants, gleaming green,
In Muslim blue ceramic pots,
Crowd upon the steps.

Walk the Jewish quarter
In the Old City.
Squeeze against the walls,
Salt-white in the sun.
Let the Fathers pass.

DIMENSIONS

A child's drawing
Of the sun
A circle marked by dips and quavers
Of an unsteady hand
Little lines radiating from its
Circumference
Like a myriad of prayers
Directed to God
Who is everywhere

An engineer's blueprint
Of a future space ship
Drawn to scale
Marked with numbers and equations
Confirmed by computers
Thrust into the heavens
To ask pardon from an all knowing God
For Adam and Eve

An old man's Bible
Opened to Genesis
Noah and the flood
The shelter of God's vow
Never again to send waters
To destroy all flesh
This shining promise throws
Its innocent light
On our latest
Nuclear reactors and
Missile sites

FLORENCE LEVER

Florence Lever at the age of 103 is Toledo, Ohio's (and perhaps the nation's) oldest living poet. Born in Southport, Lancashire, England, she grew up to become a schoolteacher. In 1911 she and her husband emigrated to the United States. They lived for a time in Utah, where she taught school before coming to settle permanently in Toledo. Her poem, "Our 50th State", won first place in the O.F.W.C. poetry contest in 1982. She particularly likes to write the Haiku form of poetry and in the years 1978-1982 published five small books of Haiku.

OUR 50th STATE

Darkness is falling on the Island,
The rolling waves, unending, meet the land;
The distant hills portend a brooding silence,
Slim palm tree fronds extend a beckoning hand.
An ancient god, tradition has it written,
Appears with flaming torch to put the night to rout,
And flare on flare beribbons all the landscape,
A conch shell's startling sound calls the devout.
Out on a jutting headland, stark against the sky,
Appears a lonely figure, lights three flares,
Pauses with hands and head uplifted in petition
That, from the ocean's depth where may lie snares,
The sea god, Neptune, will be there to guard him,
And keep the flame of courage in his heart.

HAIKU

Graceful acrobats
Squirrels jump from tree to tree
Need no safety net.

There's more eloquence
In a small child's act of love
Than great orations

The tall trees branches
Swaying in the mornings breeze
Take birds joy riding

The zest for living
Lies in tasks to be fulfilled
Compensation waits.

Wind chimes remind me
Of man's ingenuity
When carved quartz can sing.

From beneath the Earth
Life waits its resurrection
New carpets for Spring.

Intriguing shadows
Duplicate reality
Without its substance.

HAIKU

Man splits the atom
Prodigious feat of science
Meanwhile hunger stalks.

The Great Designer
Charts a course for every life
Response optional.

Shaken by March winds
Tree limbs get their exercise
Thus sap circulates.

Frustrated oyster
Transforms its irritation
Into lustrous pearl.

Happiness eludes,
Chase it and it flies away
Share, it boomerangs.

Each generous act
Merits a compensation
Down the path of life.

Sacred to each man
Is the kingdom of his mind
Where he alone rules.

HAIKU

Winter paints in white
Summer uses every shade
Green predominates.

Calibre of words
Used to sketch a verbal scene
On the screen of life.

Stay with us sunshine
Dark November days depress
Spring seems far away.

Shadows play queer tricks
Does an animal crouch there?
Beware illusions.

Ankle deep in snow
The great tree lifts up its arms
In exulatation.

Winter's artistry
Aided by no human hand
Changes the landscape.

Winter's icy winds
Chant a January dirge
June hums symphonies.

SOUTHPORT

I did not hail from London town,
    So by birth I cannot claim it;
There's a lovely spot in Lancashire,
    It's a seaside place--you name it.

With a long, wide street, and Promenade,
    And "The world's best Flower Show,"
It's a grand town, and I love it,
    For my family helped it grow.

I'll tell you the name, it's Southport,
    For its balmy air it is famed,
And days of warm, bright sunshine,
    Its attractions, too, are acclaimed.

But London town, with its landmarks,
    Which are known the wide world o'er,
Its pavements drenched in history
    Grow to mean more and more.

Let anyone mention "The Changing Guards,"
    And my eyes grow wet with tears,
For my blood is the blood of England,
    Though I've been away for years.

JOANNE NISWANDER

Joanne Niswander divides her time between music, art and writing. She is an organist and singer, a docent (tour guide) at The Toledo Museum of Art, and edits a monthly company newsletter. Her articles on family living have appeared in THE CHRISTIAN HOME, and her poems have been published in THE LYRIC, BARDIC ECHOES, HARTFORD COURANT, and WOMEN'S CIRCLE HOME COOKING.

MONUMENT TO MADISON AVENUE

They come in numbers	GIANT ECONOMY
seeking	BETTER THAN EVER
bargains and	DON'T MISS
discounts,	
paw through	HALF PRICE
markdowns,	
fill carts with	CUT RATE
merchandise and	
wait	
in	
line	
at	FOOL PROOF
cash registers	
where	SMILING COURTEOUS
automatons take	
checks,	
license numbers,	
fingerprints.	EASY CREDIT

MOVING SALE

pieces of my life
stand naked
in the sunlight

the world
comes with greedy hands
wanting
all my dreams for
a quarter

seeing only scratches
where I see

memories

GILLIES HILL, VERMONT

We sit on the deck
watching the green-black peaks
swallow up the sun

Drinks in hand
we celebrate life
laugh at memories
share our problems
and our dreams

Busy with ourselves
we do not see the mountains
creep together in the dark

Shoulders touching
they whisper their own memories
and share their dreams
for tomorrow
a million years from today

THE INN AT YESTERDAY CORNER

I stand alone beside the quiet road
That leads to nowhere; towering over me
The stately oaks, with graceful branches bowed,
Which seedlings were when first I came to be.

Long years ago the road was filled with noise
Of horses, men and wagons. Loud the sound
Would carry through the countryside, and boys,
Scarce old enough to wander, gathered round

To watch the panoply of travellers gay
And beg a hand of coppers for a smile,
Then gaze, as men and beasts would ride away,
With eyes alight and dreams to last a while.

My doors were open then, and wide to greet
The dusty traveller longing for a place
To rest a bit and then perchance to meet
Some fellow member of the human race

With whom to sing and laugh the night away
Until the dawn; then, setting out once more,
To ride the well-worn road 'til end of day
And find his welcome at another door.

My hearth is cold where once a fire's glow
Warmed hands of kings; my threshold, worn with years,
Is silent and my walls no longer know
The sound of laughter--only the salt of tears.

NURSING HOME — MA MÈRE

The thinning soles of ancient slippers rub
Across the tiles as brushes on a drum
To set the rhythm of the day for her;
A day like yesterday and yet as new
As any other one before or since.
Perhaps today will bring a new-found friend
With whom to speak and pass the hours away.
"Do you speak French?" she asks with hungry eyes
And hands eager to grasp and hold you fast.
"Alsace Loraine, the place where I was born,
So beautiful. We spoke French at home."
"What is your name? We had a bakery there
But then we came across and I am here."
Again she asks, "do you speak French?" Her eyes
Search for an answer, for a nod, or just
A touch of recognition. "Have you heard
Of Alsace, lovely place, you know, in France?"
"You speak no French? A pity, sir." She turns
To start once more the rhythm of her life
With shuffles, and a smile upon her face.

NURSING HOME — THROUGH A GLASS, DARKLY

Abandoning her cubicle of lone
She babbles to her hands. The day is like
Another, filled with this and that and so
It goes forever just a breath away.
The wheels glide hushily the whisper hall
That goes eternity and back and at
The end is still another waiting there
To carry on and out. The endless walls
Are lined with slippered feet and helpless hands
That grasp and pick and nothing. Ears untuned
To gentle hear the sweet and sense the feel
Of warming; then a hand wiping away
A mat of hair from eyes unfocused there.
The gate lets in the cool. The sun and wind
Arouse her nodding head to lift its face
And breathe a sigh. The jumbled mind delays
Its wanderings from forth and back again
To pluck an angel image from the mass
And center for a fleeting moment on
Her source of world and warm and gentleness.

THE GREENING

The greening comes
    in a night whisper
the sound rings clear
like sweetness that drips
from maples, winter-weary

The greening comes
    on the wind's breath
its warm touch stirs
the tight-closed sheath
of sleeping willow catkins

The greening comes
    with an innocent's smile
as love's freshness pours
like gentle rain
on the waiting heart.

WINTER WOODS

I came to visit you today,
Did you know?
I didn't leave a calling card,
Only my footprints in the snow.

The teasel, gentlemen in frosty brown,
Stood tall as if to guard my way
And dry star-bursts of Queen Anne's lace
Gave solemn nods to wish me good-day.

But you, my woods, I did not hear your greeting;
You did not whisper my name.
Did you, in that still, wintry silence,
Know that I came?

Perhaps in spring--and later--
When the sap begins to rise,
Then you'll nod and murmur,
And watch me with your thousand summer eyes.

A CHILD'S GARDEN OF VEGETABLES

Carrots have a way of looking
Beautiful, when they are cooking.
When the time arrives to serve them
I prefer to just observe them.

Parsley
should be used
sparsely.

Onions are most fortunate,
They think they smell like roses
'Cause God, when he created them,
Forgot to give them noses.

Luckily
I like broccoli.

Let us consider the lettuce, a head of
Which can be eaten raw, every shred of.
But lettuce, when put in a pan of hot water,
Shouldn't oughter.

O how I hate
Peas on a plate.
They never stay
But roll away.

Pickled, buttered, Harvard, plain,
Spill them and they leave a stain.
To tell the truth, beets are a pain.

Squash? Bosh!

Spinach--a vegetable known for its iron,
Quite high on the nutrition scale;
But don't feed it to me; I'd rather just eat
Some vitamin pills and a nail.

How can you tell when you pick a radish
Whether it's good or whether it's baddish?

Asparagus grows long and thin,
It has a lot of scales on.
Serve the heads with Hollandaise,
But never leave the tails on.

MAKE MINE TUTTI FRUITTI

What's the best way to pick a good melon?
Plunkin'? Pokin'? Sniffin'? Smellin'?
Reach for the nearest--there's really no tellin'.

Three cheers for the peach,
A most popular fruit;
Its marvelous flavor
I will not dispute,
But why must it have
All that fuzz on its suit?

An apple a day keeps the doctor away
So apples are banned by the AMA.

I wouldn't go bare if I were a pear.
I'd get some frilly underwear,
Put on a dress of linen rare
And get a wig of long, blonde hair.
Then folks would come to stand and stare
And say with awe: "Now, THAT'S a pear!"

Grapes in a bunch (I have a hunch)
Chatter incessantly when out to lunch.

Bananas are yellow, bananas are green,
Bananas are brown and all shades in between.
Green ones are chewy, yellow ones mello,
But dark brown bananas are squishy as jello.

I have a question--now don't think I'm dumb--
Is a plum a young prune or a prune an old plum?

Straw, razz, black, blue,
Cran, goose, elder too,
Raw, cooked, snack, dine,
Pie, jam, salad, wine.
Berries are a favorite of mine.

Pineapple, pineapple, under your skin
How can I tell what shape you are in?

Rhubarb pie is so delicious
And they say it's quite nutritious,
Keeps you regular and healthy,
Makes the rhubarb farmer wealthy.

Cherries sweet and cherries sour,
They all taste just grand;
But the ones I like the most
Are the chocolate covered brand.

CASE 13 (BROWN vs GREEN)

I never could understand with clarity
How there could ever be such disparity
Between the folks who like their bananas green
And those who want them brown so hardly any yellow can be seen.

Pity the grocer, trying to please the shoppers many
Who want only green bananas when there aren't any
Or else the people who (with bananas they eat the spots of),
Shop only on days when bananas green he has lots of.

I wonder if it would be a fallacy
For each store to have this policy:
"Monday for brown, Tuesday for green,
Buy the other shades days in between."

Because, when it comes to banana buying,
It's very trying.

IF NOSES COULD HEAR
(for Sara)

Wouldn't it be funny
If noses could hear
And when you had a cold
You'd wipe your ear?

Wouldn't it be funny
If feet could talk
And your mouth got tired
When you went for a walk?

Wouldn't it be funny
If fingers could see
And you'd use your eyes
To hold a cup of tea?

Wouldn't it be funny
To brush your head
And lay down your teeth
When you went to bed?

But isn't it wonderful
Shoulders can shrug,
Toes can wiggle,
Arms can hug,

Eyes can wink
And lips can kiss
To tell you I love you
JUST LIKE THIS!!!

WINSTON SMITH

Winston Smith is a retired schoolteacher and a pilot who writes poetry. He lives in Lost Peninsula, that isolated bit of Michigan on Toledo's northern border. His poems have appeared in MODERN MATURITY, MARK, THE PLOW, BEND OF THE RIVER, and several local anthologies.

THE OLD MAN AND THE ANTS

Old man withered and withdrawn from all
the world's delight
shuffling along your narrow stretch of sidewalk
tremulous but intent
stalking the scurrying ants.
Summerday after summerday, resenting
I sat on the porch steps of boyhood watching
the daily destruction of the ants
your old man's shoes-
high sided, leather split and broken
resoled with thick leather that would outlast you
every other step or so descending
not just content to crush, but to erase
with final callous twist of foot.
Old man in your denial of lesser forms of life
I doubt you ever saw me watching you, old man
with a faded denim shirt buttoned
high about your scrawny neck
coat and wrinkled pants hung loose upon you
not too large-
but rather you withered beneath them.

THE WIND

I never saw the wind, but still
I met it one day on a hill
A little wind come frolicking
an innocent and artless thing
tossing flowers as it came
alone, attendant on its game.

I never saw the wind, but yet
on a hillside one day we met
a little wind without a care
that came on me all unaware
and paused a bit to gently place
cool curious fingers on my face.

They say the wind's invisible
but yet one day upon a hill
a little wind and I did meet
It came and went on lightsome feet
and up the hill where it did pass
left waving footprints in the grass.

FLY IN AMBER

Time turns on
a trick of heaven
where paling stars blink out

beneath my feet
the dawn dark road
echoes to
a thud of steps
and seconds blot
the turning page.

A barren road
past meager snow
on drifted leaves
and darkness huddled dying
under naked trees.

The road retreats
and I move on
the paling stars are gone.

***

Baltic Amber
in blue earth
buried in the sea
wash and scour
of wave and tide
work to set it free.

Search along the beaches where
in myriads of sand
rare pieces lie

golden fossil resin
translucent
in the light
within
a liquid moment
from an age ago.

On time trapped
fragile wings
such a glittering.

TWO JUNCOES FLEW

round the mountain ash
this morning
in out about
black and white
among the branches
where red berry clusters hung.

One chasing other
love by lover
never quite to capture
careless rapture
circling round
the tree.

To the window
close by me
saw the fickle flight of one
flung against
hard transparency

By breath dimmed glass
lay hid
what fell below
into the careless grass.

One Junco flew
round the mountain ash
this morning
a time or two
and searching found
only bare branches
with red berry clusters hung.

TRUE POET

Do not tamper lightly
with the dawn
for wonder of
what words prevail
when Venus dims
hung pale above
the coming light.

Find words
that spun slow rise
from wrack
of shattered night
to limn
the risen light.

Dawn dazzled words
opalescent framed
for colors
tint and hues
that rise and rage
unnamed
to fade before
the gathered light.

FLASHBACK

Interstate
75
rides the heaped up hogback
of earth, strides
across the old south city
and dams the thwarted streets
where I look down to see...

Time
leaching from red bricks
of old buildings
staining the ambient air
along a stagnant street
with mezzotints
of sun and shade.

Queer quirk
to trigger so uncalled
this vivid flash
from buried deep
in twists and turns
of me.

Riffling through
the layered years
to an early page
where walking
I should meet
myself again
on a younger street.

OLD CANAL HOUSES

Upriver-down
traffic sluices
through maumeetown
on a concrete trail
of hectic flow
bottleneck
of come and go
runnel for
rush hour spates
greenlightspurts
red-light-waits.

Along the way
and slow to die
old wood houses
stranded by
this alien tide
ride the berm
a ruined row
relics from
an age ago.

of twenty-some
to note and know
abandoned one
that draws me so
with empty windows
forlorn stare
out at something
no longer there.

Could it be-
when traffic shuns
the trail at night
to spin a spell
by thin moonlight
across the age-worn
threshold there

-to turn
to the sound
of a boatman's horn
and through windows old
when I was born-

look out to see
erie waters
where a road
would be.

DUSTY ANSWER

Walked through
empty downtown
sunday streets
searching everywhere
for the cenotaph
of whats not there.

---Saw only
printed paper
blowing on the wind
and a lonely
passing car
bearing sabbath souls
impervious
under glass.

Wandered all
that mottled day
adding up
the blacks and white
and found the sum
was gray.

SING JOHNNY ONE NOTE

Black on gray
black on gray
soft soot black
on wash of gray

stark black trees
no trace to see
where slow spring green
still waits to be

gray clouds this day
from dawn to dark
no crack of blue
no sun sneaks through

trees a trace
of soot black lace
maze of twigs
on soft cloud gray

all a tree
can do is be
black-
black on gray

today.

DAMSEL FLIES ARE FOUND

Where Osiers grow
and shade lies deep.
I know
one serried stand
that keeps
a summer covenant
of sheltered green
when sun's a hot
and angry eye
that stares down from
a sirocco sky.

When witless blows
my windy world
around mortality
I go in search
of sanity
where Osiers grow
and time suspends
a windless place
where damsel flies
implausibly
beat gauzy wings
through dim eternities.

ELEMENT OF PURPLE

Liaison of red and blue
Tyrian tint of kings
common hue to clover
purple presence coloring
in the list of things.

Juices bursting on the tongue
from ripe Catawbas
Damascus plums
excitement stirred in subtle wines
by rain and sun among the vines

substance lent to shadows
imperative of violets
glints in air
round black unbound
and wind tossed hair

urgent
in the pulsing murmur
of the sovereign sprint
of blood

purple comment
on lightning's flash
muttered by the thunder

banshee wail of a fleeing train
running down an iron trail
across a purple night.

DAY WITH APPLES

Contemplate
the core of apples
consider all the gnawed remains
- and the multitude of days
and wonder
what is left
what is left
after all the fluid days
gutter down relentless drains.

Count the days
like apples
eat the days
like apples
sweet ripe summer apples
all the careless apples
that burden summer's tree
- find how fall
diminishes
what seemed
infinity.

Mark the ways
of apples
frost struck winter apples
sparse upon the tree -
stark as
contemplation
of the end
of days.

Heatherdown Press   3450 Brantford Road   Toledo, Ohio   43606